T0279184

Bumblebees

Also by Deborah Meadows

Bumblebees

Lecture Notes, a duration poem in twelve parts

The Demotion of Pluto: Poems and Plays

Three Plays

Translation, the bass accompaniment: Selected Poems

Saccade Patterns

How, the means

Depleted Burden Down

Goodbye Tissues

involutia

The Draped Universe

Thin Gloves

Growing Still

Representing Absence

Itinerant Men

"The 60's and 70's:

from The Theory of Subjectivity in Moby-Dick"

Bumblebees

Deborah Meadows

ROOF BOOKS
New York

Copyright © Deborah Meadows 2024

ISBN: 979-8-9896652-5-9
Library of Congress Control Number: 2024940157

Cover photo with permission: Hawthorne Valley Farmscape
Ecology Program, Ghent, NY

Book design by Deborah Thomas

NEW YORK | Council on This book is made possible, in part, by the New
STATE OF | the Arts York State Council on the Arts with the support
OPPORTUNITY.
of Governor Kathy Hocul and the New York State Legislature.

Roof Books
are published by Segue Foundation
300 Bowery Fl 2
New York, NY 10012
seguefoundation.com

For book orders, please go to Roofbooks.com

Dedicated to Howard

Contents

Ant Hills

Our recent look at how humans inhabit time
disintegrates to images, smoke curling from chimneys,
idea of anteroom, practice of porch.

We drew a box to site windows.

We received no answer when hospitalized, no birthday
or grandkids.

Your face wiped off readily, your phone sends itself
a message, makes a demand, comes loose.

Here's a paper white narcissus you can't dance to, text as
texture, facture: defeated by a bug, late in the game.

What comes next?

Some used walks to resolve a mess by elimination,
but when no one was there: caught on a cam,

uploaded hits, archived, retrieved, alienated, infested, nearly
extraterrestrial in its being, barely carbon-based.

Breathing is a way to tell, life support,
tree-respiration and out, so we play in cardboard boxes
appliances come in, visit structure in our mind.

A taller ant hill to snooze through mentally, a house
where we once lived, plans we drafted for one unbuilt
where we won't enjoy rooftop open-air.

Red without sheathing, hang it on the wall: totemic past,

a reduced ornament, our need for stairs, the concealed
page out back.

Letter came, no reply made sense, zipped shut. The way
out of the hive is not the way inside, stuck with oxbow
shape, makes no sense, jingled small change. Price

charged against us, scalloped by wind, patterned—
neither bomb blast nor sea breeze fenced
out Thor, his offspring, but pond-side:

egrets, twilight, diapers, diopter count, soft shoe,
do the whooping crane, moon walk, asemic writing

hardly stuff of family memories, emotive engines, cultured
story of belonging within those parameters.

Bumblebees

Try exultation: *n.* a state of rising or expanding in fierce opposition to awe, that silver necklace encrypting dangerous love.

We faced the truth.

A passage a person writes not once but sub-canonically; we stew paper, plant fiber, and power lines, noncommittal ones, one-offs 'enough already.'

Dexterity of visual recognition: likeness by likeness, profile as hatched electronic time-keeper's content, rough sketch, Conté crayon hat addition—last minute.

As lost as lost in a Mongolian sandstorm buries all we know of wind pattern, all pedagogical routes to legacy camp, our usual spot for hot tea, cool down.

We are salted with rotated figures excised from pre-existing works, reference in hiding, unspecified complaint, part human, fabled justice, a call to light, averages.

We broke the silence.

We misread anguish as threat, flail for oxygen as attempted
assault, taken down, wounded.

Warhead accidentally slipped to the Mediterranean Sea, then
upon rescue effort, we fumbled it lower, unreachable trophy,
case deterioration.

We installed temporary art in the park from thrown out
materials to disrupt continuity of hatred in the community,
to heal.

We had a crazy hunch how things so heavy got here, disturbed
bones, patterned thought, quarried first causes, harp recordings.

Power lines in the city-edge plant we hacked just coming
online, restoration play, just king of electrical charges,
juice suspended.

We picketed, not to violate the code, Nuremberg, not to bomb
the open market in Guernica, Spain, not to have allies violate
the principles in Palestine.

Please Respond, Break Silence.

Shatter body mass indexed to vibratory scale of electric guitar, no excess to subtract as teetering beauty of form makes us.

Declaration of royal status, old shameless table lamp as scepter, ivy vines our scalp, our soprano Brittens it all, drinks peasant wartime water.

We cry a hitch in their ethics, or itch in their thicket amounts to the same thing, give away per dose of identity, slip of their cover narrative, say, or speech recognition.

If we were born with full ability in mathematics, would our grandparents' suffering shape tatters overcome in a later electronic, spliced age?

We pointed: here is a child who added to after-school book club intelligence quotient but lived in a bird's nest wedged between barbed wire like ordinary mortals.

Strollers push precious strollers past us, another currency,
not nation we trust, in service to service, waged, wagered,
bundled away.

End of a circle, we say, carved into whole hills, bypassed circuit
with new definition drafted in vestigial language, possibly legal
recourse to shirk.

Freaky velocity unites our degraded bits, syllabic jabs, coded
senders, locator moves for dance floor derivative role, yet could
it counter rapacious greed, extractive subjectivity?

We rang brass bells, imposed alert to cells, index finger to
sluice, juice to croak frogs along pathogenic ambition, tried a
compassionate canary's suffocation.

For the justice challenged, we rejected coming home in a sack,
cloth-of-the-devil sold as specialty yardage come due, geriatric
snake in voltage surge.

We had less integrity than scribal output of The Copyist, monk inset with ambition, scorch mark, workload excess. We raised falcon.

Less atmosphere on Mars, our flight possible added lift, capital city lined up, recharged, tangerine miniaturization plots, our good health cratered.

We questioned the meaning of cowboy of the autoclave, bully-tooters, blank, banked out, wrong tyrant size.

Front tooth embedded diamond be both vulgar and refined extinction, our whims headed for, varied by re-telling.

Simple line, we become sexually charged on and in there just a thought of its sympathetic vibe between, won't be on the page.

Bee urgency zigzag and brush up against us like, brash consideration overpayment, we hear you, all of you, in recordings, have purchase on them, not in the wires.

Adrenal worries our plural form: charcoal overdrawing confused first draft, dear shoeless neighbor, chemical durability soon enough.

But *the garden*, "We, the gardeners, do in our intuitive upkeep, low water design, plant for pollinators and butterflies, plain and fancy equal under the law ...

We made proto-transfer with patient packet boat, unwitting nuclear scatter, chug against sufficient frictional waters healed.

Have half haven breathy for we bounce our cadence: yeah yeah antiquated liminal tongue.

We recited times' provisional choral contingent funding standard over trumpet fixture ominous hum. No use!

We glow again then: chocolate precedes death and rain clouds, too—up thrust, slip, and other kind, force in measurable time, cracked life, crackpot alphabet.

We carried nothing extra in going on, on and on, but superfluous artistic forking virulent form took.

Scale perforated object, leaf-drop is temporary quorum, stay.

Carried Away: an account of bumblebees exalted by utter beauty of nature (vol. 1)

We adapted our press, Roycrofters a rarity, communal soup refined the style, yet visitors, authors, political radicals of their time, word got out.

Flavored by mineralized volcanic soils, we wakened savor, our accomplice unknown; interiors stage dialog in strange places tangentially referred to here with a gate out of here.

Imagine an hour, hear our digital thermometer, our false satisfaction, fumbled it, sorry; we exchange large segment with difference encoded.

We pretend body fronts other body, refracted purpose, bones of it, shudder-worth, they crack, played at being lions, beauties, absolute.

Breach thought: attentive then suspended, suspense as enfolded physical blanket-state, please use the place we left behind, tend the animals, You-many, caring.

Everything on the outside skin.

Everything runs on inner life.

We cannot know their thoughts, their fluids, no ultimate meaning, text, location-shift.

Leisure again, our recumbent bicycle way, subsoil surviving
when ignored best, stakes pulled by tension in tiebacks, we
collapse, crumple fabric, prior existence.

Somewhat unlikely, we had to stand a long time, misquoted
again but colorfully editioned, removed spill from seabirds
carefully, shelter fund.

We knew that frail thing wouldn't endure as fragment, sang
along with car radios.

Bass line joy instills you, damaged thing, goofy outfit over it all.

Made up cause, we said unexpectedly, put it back together
again, ground borders to sausages for divergent cats in a strike
for impurity.

We were sporting kilometers.

Iroquois here for a long time, *in situ* hypothesis prevails; we
had evidence both linguistic, archeological— Point Peninsula
pottery decoration, rocker stamp to corded.

Thanks for the gifts, Planet, long distance gift exchange.

We shared refuge outside the village: no need for kivas, bark
cloisters.

Role of genetic diversity in our lowered spread of disease, our
mixture lowered unease, some captive claim to stay.

Client of the colony, we knitted kin ties important, strike
dances held, no redress.

We made terrible mistakes, got off the train at the wrong stop, miscalculated how much our earth could take.

Maintenance of vision is marking our minds as we convene a forest of signs and get on.

We ignored how our partings are married to the word "all" as so much logic-filler lost in the igneous grind.

When superstition fell across science, we got up the nerve.

When a little girl went on strike, we got up to shout, threw off chains, made a growl recovered here.

We knew percentages were not high enough for peer-worthy takes, our dynamic stall not by flock: emergent animal behavior liked for leaderless simple rules, wind pattern.

Grow the means to see those outside the expanding lasso of "we" to be close to our heart, empathic to difference, with difference, repair.

Stray cats run miles to return to their snow monuments.

Wouldn't you run miles to come back? And wouldn't you feed the movie poster, kiss it twice for animism's sake? Don't let it see us when we're doing it; replication wants privacy.

We were an echo chamber for thought. We were profiled, caricatured. We had sing-song cadence, nonsense questions, character.

Distribution scale of landscape we move through in a show of our comparative anatomy. We clunked against idols.

Impressed against our will, got-up idea of having one, they came for our grain. But unseen underground: our cassava, yam, potato, fallback against short winter light.

By overly taxing efforts, tight pants, and flimsy blouse we knew migratory season as vast expenditure of heat, magnetic reckoning, humble twig.

We ate unquestioningly when fully incorporated without wings, marked ghostly, our consubstantial theme almost free of disgust.

Is this another gift stolen from slaves: long chain polymers for self-quenching fire, precious jet fuel additive?

Prometheus dominated by Unworthies of Dow Chemical?

Absurd lives answer fumbled effort, our landmarks mere
cultural relics of ignored earth, left-alone outcropping, slip
plate totem, inactive saber tooth cat zone.

Back there, we stored pataphysical laughter: de-braining jokes,
push up chemic answers to sewer remittance, ring around
pratfall authors.

Our aerial water drops preserved forests of egret, seashells,
thrown out sound sounding, solo folded down word-cornered
globe, root countenance opaque no longer.

Desire in terms of exploration: we came to over depend on
heat shields, surely a mark of their success, and equipped with
piscine visual filters, we thrilled to neon nights at sea.

With or without conchology grid, we had Murex beauty;
we began to study warming, acidifying of their ancestral site,
ventriloquism.

We didn't need squirrels to learn how to chatter; we followed our conscience.

Thigh-deep we face the sea's extent: good primates like us groom, spell, frame retreat as *The Sentinels of No Outer Point*.

Unsatisfied by any particular location, our strange dislocation crowded the concept of journey as field leveled for all comers.

We were just walking. Walking was never transparent.

Fractional distillation of water, not the harmless material of cloud-watchers such as we walking here, soon to join cyclonic force, uproot, spread wide.

We were named *Hardly a Genealogical Wonder* meaning nature's pollinators afield; we are daughters, sons of zesty protoplasm and leftover spunk from our egg-headed galaxy.

We failed as penitents; we made excuses, got lost, were late, meant well, forgot, were misled, had to work, took to the road, gave in too easily.

Elegance: we were elegant in gray silk shirts over black pants in movement, arms flexing, wind on wheat field, our green green grass of home.

These weren't rehearsals for the event but second last beds, a wager to imagine the walk down River Road all the way to the Good-Bad bridge, no longer there.

Defenseless in sleep, we each become an ego, desirous; acousti-
cal measures of being sound me out, hold me to your ear, sea
roar.

Attracted to unknown regions, our consent to distance read
symbolically, music's segment, provisional study yet to be filled
in.

Grooves of blarney recorded on 78s, obsolete, not the oldest
form, Saint Louis, Louis, curious for grown world, restless, we
ignited a mime troupe, truth without speech.

Once out of the carrying case, our flakes, pet rocks, how they
came here, why they have to go, scientific evidence, kings and
mushrooms.

Look, by sea approach how pregnant Keros reclines Cycladic-
style; that's one version rising from our old trial, homing in,
mineral pigment flaked by time.

But *the garden*, flight paths, sourced succor, clear water mapped
our minds up to now.

Formative Period

Left with contemplative surplus, supposed tricky finger,

proposed rafters might look into pattern settled, for now,

as law, saw there graphic tables, indices: loose riddle,

double entendre worked out puzzle of existence if lawn

cells click before the Learned were learning, before

mentored gaze, conversed at lunch, a gift of attentive time.

Then erased files stand in for your old car in relation

to empty streets, provisional cave, not entirely unmarked

drank deeply, nay quaffed to slake it for Time,

its relation to travel, language, cure, far away from

darker side of persistence, crazed Obstinate in moral

frame descending, claw released from errantry's

perimeter, spinning child, once vacated trained dancer,

scrap trailing on string, scrap elevating with centrifugal

force, growth invites ice core centuries, lack,

appointment system, dismay at reversal, left with

Led Zep memory-worm, driven shoulder to hip way,

chord compression mastered in basement

with someone's brother, perfected arrow analogy,

audible practicum for tiny expanse covered phrase

at a time, then Monday. Phosphorescent watch face

discharged nighttime location, second sweep tending

hand on a move to fold another plane ever-green, ever-

commercial if you discount nonlinear space where we

live most of the time. Initial it done to another,

done not fair, love or peace, thumbs up or down ranked

vote for middling talent tally-ho damage, equine

progress granted an enviable future, musky,

expensive, flat as proverbial flatness, and yet chip wafer

thinness aside there might be much less to pack onto one

pack mule in service, cast in dream as unlikely passerby

recognition shamed to a still, then big laugh, flopped

scene over—we're here back together again faded green

glow where we import history pre-fabricated, each

square an eighth of the height-length of the whole,

architecture promised uplift from mud furrowed lives

that keep us going year after year, chromo-sky

at university library, structure or more feeling

for structure? Animal movement observed as holy day

regularity, procession, turned by line's end when not

enjambed shoulder to knuckle ratio, thus turned in

season pass for entry to everything from International

Klein Blue to Vantablack and back, each migration, self-

consoling Simone Forti bear-movement, variation on

scheme floored a zoo, pose as duration, drafted from

angles sort out temporal terms, takes a long time to

produce one, several studies, four to a page, say, stylized

cut-outs, an all-seeing cyc, visible scene on another

plane just behind improvised so-called plan, free waters

replaced by stolen, precarious piece joined to shelter

piece, crate, calendric technology, governance of bodies,

free-standing lollipops, wall work in crates, lines

wrapped with lines, a sort of language of architectural

plans corroded by overwritten horizons, draft elevations,

open space, Frederic Rzewski's minimal piano plinked

falling rain, entangled farmed or farmer, famed fungal

spores, antidote to theories of sublime experience,

dangerous heights, soaring ego-capped mount, yet down

at the base we mailed draft essays, exuberant voice

came across, lifted up, made *artists* the talk to have,

between continents and time, mystery of how distant tip

communicates vitality, danger, light across distance,

filament mycelia, one face swapped for another, at war

with language antonym, metric synonym, nighttime

cameras surveil deer, smuggler, pack animals, border

theme, perforate two fabrics to join distich by hand, yet

actuated by ear, we enter the picture, its craggy

mountains, huts for those with walking sticks, hard

to take time for half-life of uranium, artist-made

photograms with pieces of it, no sunlight: here's a plant

that draws out contamination, heals damage, O Tree!

Awoke

from default mode to wonder brain, all gets set aside, all

is here, as ever, how did we miss guitars? Gate for you

to be, help from amateur cultivators, milkweed,

bandaged help, bundled from harm, emptiness, wait-

jumper right here, light having traveled so far from

extinction. Clay armature, clay collapse, willow fuzz

floats backlit in breeze, but shelling continues over

there; Los Angeles postcards Sandow Birk made during

closures, dystopic elements in old time

chromolithograph, pinkish at first promotional glance,

our palm trees' promise, further out from war ruins kids

played among is Phyllida Barlow, birds return through

effort, monarchs, too, effort at coral health, rehabilitated

human posture, mint, green onions, budding place

modifier, nothing to say but vocalize just to feel

vibratory life attach to skein of star life.

Narrow Leads

Monitor, an obedient relative, please listen: our

dreaded fresh stills, grain blockade, wage theft

tech giant anti-maneuver inflected it with fear,

outnumbered mavens shush new person's item

worked figures, stung tough, stoical to the end.

I was hurt. You were hurt. We were hurt.

Why hate? There's love right beside you.

Our journey begins where gondola lifts end,

shuddered transfer of momentum stoppages,

rugged range calls *come closer*, see around

sight itself, triangular pool of light ajar, not

what suffragists suffered jail for you to have

squandered, taken away, re-districted. Unmade

works, we slipped past rock hard renunciation

as an improbable mode, basic right delineated

text found in Wayback machine, vertical curse

on desperate theft, we crave connection, selfies

at demonstrations, sound very "theatre," broad

caste, near the bottom, dogs hide from lightning,

sponges from solitude, druids from end times

situated henge with non-henge, pitiable topos

collected cast-offs curbside, tactical plot,

beautiful answer, wit, global friction, stricture

abolition, rallied rights, separate yet find our

way back to a practice, pick up guitar and knit.

Understory

An image emerges from torn issues settled long ago.

Deliberate puzzle yet plotless. Motivated and looped

as if that cures a modernist impulse to signal raven

intellect, their poetry a shadowed soul, time

a compression bandage when cuts go deep, aid

in the form of wordless method, two shades this

side of instinct, immediate as imagination and

nearly as disturbing.

        Meaty in the way organs by

Altoon comic-shift with spacing, color, flopping

free, as if being made is easy, *Hello, etc.*, squishy

reasoning, to be human, an inner monolog, one that

becomes enormous as a cloud whose forward edge

folds back on itself, creaturely life with handwriting—

carbonized roll of prophetic agony, for what?

                        Marks

precede concocted room, tongue clipped for

de-mythifying our hero's ball-court body who spoke

out on pain, dared disfigure perfect silence simply

here, primal stone in volcanic gray.

                                          Actors' lines

excised for time constraints: Outplay the Lords of

Xibalba? Sure. Hey, melonhead, give us a spit before

the match-up. You can do a lot of damage with that

thing. Come here and give it to me. An entire national

ethos? I didn't have an opinion on the matter.

It repulsed me. Flesh and bones, sanctified food,

food in turn again. I didn't have much luck with plants.

Losing teams were sacrificed slowly this time.

Hey, put them to rest already, can't take it. Without

using the word, it was a study of evil.

                                          They'll be

left with scars. Willow flycatchers become displaced:

without two miles of continuous forest canopy,

cowbirds sleaze into their nests. Forest understory,

diligent cattle pervasive, heat pattern neoclassical

as being separable from world, secondary ache

comes with followed instruction, ordered free,

meaning saddled by described scene: we learned

to read currents, shoals, attentive without anxious

refrain, too young to know broken record's sound,

grief and war, low-to-middling self-knowledge,

                              Are

you philosophizing against thinness of layers,

bothness, stoniness, then the outer ring, its

simple petal structure, mutual aid shouldered there

under a fascist storm front, its own end. How

licking that bloody wound on your arm could

be considered a mild form of cannibalism, carved

stone glyph now extruded plastic figurine.

Pollen Situations

left the tried path of here and back,

here and back, not enclosed

self-sufficient island, flight from here to

big slab of aggression, here music tempers

takeover, burnouts on 6th Street Bridge,

body and property, public work over

transversal tracks, drainage channel posing

as river, someone squatting against skyline

of extractive corporate headquarters, movement

while waiting, itinerant men, not ways

to preserve but simply create singular time

with word-order, somehow defies tradition

of calligraphy, typographic play, some glow

in the dark, tripped over words, helicopter

into human heat signature, same by growth

crystallized form, how Hong Kong artists

code umbrellas against gas, when the old

guys were young, tentative, parodic quest

tick summer grass and woodlands, old

threat new injustice, prying social worker,

invasive property flipper, 294 page LA river

master plan thrown municipal sink exuberant

foot traffic sensuous August night air,

iced drinks laughter looked-into scheme,

flimsy example of remnant language.

Exiled Poets

pollen studies, adherent, how a venerated syllable placed you in
the world, proximate history to philosophy worry

old hived ancestors, carved to be ruin, overcome habit

of poetry, structure near upper property line, affinity to hexago-
nal cell, assistant

librarian shelved against head boss, moths to flames

done wrong, pollen provoked endless commentary

Mushroom Identification

gill structure, spore pattern on paper

captive by rescue intention
false floor, clock tower

made wholesome, tar removal
one at a time, then good enough

to release to the sea again,
how new water's density, free

nut held out to the veteran, his
rural brethren, never tamed or

turned, drawing student drawing
water, water all around, sound stage

assembled for one night only,
Exclusive!

muffled protest against mufflers,
the muffler-class, its guard force

overly precious, false victim,
a missing preposition stands out,

underground band slipped out without
truth or justice, lush bird life makes

estuary all the better, our bodies,
mental work, activist effort by spring,

later: passed a long line of deer hunters,
Sunday of opening season, but quiet!

voice actor's door, calumny of tone,
breached surface, away—
beside *congueros*, guardians of tradition,
innovative blend, shoulder-drop

upon dance beat back-step,
          up on going forth

hip sway, seemingly arisen at night—
favored insect here in good standing,

contributor of wealth, mass action,
ability to read pollen situations,

failed by vaudeville, fluent author, yet
product skinned, prepared, suspended

recognition, partial hologram, didn't
make each other a brand, historic

consciousness, a singular look at one's
condition, rather baby talk buzz, does street

Restorations

bird claws walk overhead
on opaque glass, beak sharpening
rhythm

wild horses of Washoe Lake
make familial a world of
autumn grass, rabbit brush

plastic rock, sub-stations
stair tread repair
as it lay, false messiah collection,

hoard of unworn items,
bins on wheels, Oz voice-
over, limited, those set phrases,

flat ponderous reasoning
simple to mail, to award

rotation of rangeland,
roles in jagged past rubbed
up against, all misread

a lover's body's sustain pedal
against cessation,
a trail of helium gas follows
behind our planet, too light
for our atmosphere to hold

incarceration reforms
Quaker effort, continuity

Frankfurt School thought
against consumerism, then
without anticipation shopping
malls die one by one

sincere in our ironic rejoinders
to such a screwed-up world
depleting our lovely earth?

blue things, thought
made with cardboard again

sub-vocalizing up to
full on wailing:
daughter loss, I was
dreamin'.

warm towel on bird
fallen to ground, at four
hours eyes open, then
another hour, it flew.

Native American land
rights, rewilding, bison
antibiotic-free

vagabonding, not keep
a house, translate
from spry languages,
transfer of
properties, sheet music
signed copy

dispersal pattern,
survival rate, evidence

of bumblebee play,
its own end, color,
ball court,

bumblebee inventions
symbols to inhabit,
our team, scent our locale.

intense relations kept
unresolved, kept in play,
held in our mind for
now, sort of destiny
no longer
iterated as task, but
as configuration: we

why an insect collective,
that collaborator

ravens, more ravens,
more nouns, spontaneous biotic
crush of language.

Try collage.
Drop lava.
Scram rabbit.
Mar lenses.
Part stems.
Lap rupture.

Three Stones

1. from top of the kids' slide: destiny in mild form

2. opening comments in unreadable scrim

3. effect: muffled trumpet bell

fondness for slow change, wearable art,
wistful on time,

                            illusions
of one's significance in ratio to quanta
of propaganda, Achilles' achievements,

self as his mythic sweat band,

love's quizzical mutual regard

Esplanade City

mange, injuries on mountain lion P-22
car culture, in-breeding

Never knew what fell outside genetic purview

ignored under lawn furniture
paintings done by animal-people who kept running

collaborate in hippodrome of satiric gross-out's,
gouged history

go faster, pass on the left, chronic field for now,
temps,

esplanade city our lion couldn't shake off—
we're not a set of raindrops on his coat

wild bees can make it where right
things are, or better, left alone.

How adapted instruments' sly tone ...

to coat those innards prepared
to seek your look at intimate extruded
pearl, your ah-ha, let go, hear song's hook,
shimmy a command performance for now

we flash our compound eyes
use an accent most find urbane
given intense phrasing, heterodox
aversion to Aristotelian thought

our mummers erase distinctive
regional vowel fortitude, tongue
to hiss, load-ready to roll off
an anther, snake eyes

saying it says: come inside
it's quiet

heavy ideological centuries
but not *only* ideological
per Stuart Hall, not
exhaustively, more to study

apocryphal sea crossing
theory jubilee
influence recognized now
as confluence

antihistamine, state's foot
on the neck, parlance of force
emblem of sudden terror,
syntax-free: cobweb or gunsight,

just passing by
just passing through
Petrarchan rye fields

snow-covered cars,
tombstones under Buffalo
street lights,
no ha-ha here
we remember, yes, we do

project a hominid future, carry bag
into projected future,
tools, numeracy, tomorrow
and tomorrow

Insect Digs

Line to forest where enough contour about
will you be?

Why wouldn't leaves, animal fur, rock pile
make for our hidden nest? Burrow gently into
this good night, world workers …

mudslide over prehistoric conquest, digs,
unearthed plein air sex, evidential fiber

We read a recipe for lemon after-lives,
Lebanon orchards we tend.

How to inhabit her travel case on wheels?
Refugio strand gulls banking in relation
to photographers.

Those long noodles paired our friends
in a shock of violence this Lunar vigil.

A test of emerald hills, ceanothus
bloom, California laurel, cancer-free.

Down here null, nullity is ok for a line
where rupture could measure quanta
of light, desire to figure it out, figure forth.

Cobalt extraction for kids: we dug
Congo *artisanal* (weasel word) mines.

On screen consumer palace: high
impulse alert, pollen for *sleek torso fit*

and then a little later, it all came undone.

Mismatched Heteronymic Plurality

how much thought after all these years

imagined sea caves before actual

perform nothing of the kind

itch balanced on a quiver of flesh

primed for slowdowns, hesitations,

shuddered on a sharp turn to loud task

not a final journey or a daily turn

no stray hair near appetitive time that

repeats without explanation, less perfect

than just-about finished

vocation of cuts and stitches, how an oval,

as the first in step-by-step, can build

to a cartoon portrait, our example

preferred in jaunty pairs, sly with

dry observation, human foible,

anything too slow to see additive

direction as previous landform—gravel

bed, sanded smooth, prior life as upright

monument to a preposterous time, pre-alluvial

to say the least, flows collapse, between

refuge and promontory: a few dozen

of our readers, couple of pages of squares

where we blink and shift, comb behind

the moment of response, *same as yours*

and on to a new idea and on to an old

idea, and on …

The Curiosities of Janice Lowry

1. The Wedding

                    And as for
this box, the big carrot speaks
but fell to silence.
          Fall.
          Falls.
Freeze-frame nostalgic, or lack
of strong feeling not depicted?

There's the girl with a big O
over her left eye

tethered to an empty boat.

Cross-section of house,
a slice really, life as silhouette
          (earlier century?)
particulars rubbed black
perimeter has many vicious pins: pearl-topped
fish in "attic," a turquoise heart over genitals
wedding dress remnant fit tight
assemblage box all bunched up,
old tape measure

2. *Janice Lowry's Studio*

post-rupture
worktable: fiber masks for atomized
                              paint

early iterations punctuate

petty by size, roof line
could be Constantinople holy man
tall hat, white beard,
Santa mitts hold tray:
look, a dancing infant!

another recess between pilasters:
tar baby & Kermit-green
Billy goat

Night scene: black, blackened
heart, white egg

tempura ingredients ≠ human form

3. *Side Show*

game of skill or chance?
side-show (county fair, old time)

marbles at rest
stay at rest

clown comes out: its path in the style
of a cuckoo clock; door opens
on the hour from the abdomen of youth

"coo-coo, coo-coo," it cries

flanked by urns
an arc or web says "territory,"
says "target for strikes"

come ball-throwers
come chance, do your best

4. *Past Present + Future*

maintenance daily:

bird cage remnant, rust
over ultramarine blue (flocked with
                         Cornell stars?)
Is that white bordered holy-card
of her, of She?

butter stamp attached there
red heart topped by flame
          "Sacred Heart of M."

we serialize butter pats
over
and over
                    Unbroken
chicken egg lashed
to front,   right
where we used to remove
tray each day
          where we used to pray
"do not let her fly away"
a vertical lance
pierces our chicken egg shell.
                Forgive them.

5. Where Is The Bottom

my blinking doll:
inner works revealed

eyeball with thread hole
out round back

raw things, raw doll
paint-flaked hammer handle
topped by iron marble
(post-Industrial cornhusk doll?)
            3 remnants:
folding ruler 3½ - 6¼ inches
                    19 – 20 inches
                    20 – 21¾ inches

scrapped cross-piece,
Commie red star
on perforated wheel

Our box is gilt-edged,
inside: reverse subtracted blue
            fragmented red
            chipped white

6. *Listen* and *In the Beginning*

recto: lashed chicken egg
over illegible egg shape

verso: black with white dots,
        butter stamp head, baby doll arms,
lashed white egg body

deliquescent Baby Book of _____
                                    name
date of birth
length
weight
boy or girl
hair color
eye color

vaccination schedule

7. *Night Talk*

—servers—

utensil handle (wood) serves
nicely as cosmic tree

egg for sock darning (did you mend
the hole?)

dog-girl paddles forward
levitates with assistance of
red stick over old homes,
says, "Howdy!"
to red, yellow, green bird

two
interlocking diamonds

grab that pointed stick
mostly for its orb
just above torn horizon

8. *Prince Albert*

Phoenix stamp
U.S. Mail "times" five

dripped resin for hinged
frame, edged by faux-shark
                                                    teeth

Cereus giganteus, 1959 [iconic cactus]

Prince Albert
a duck contained

What's in your pail, little girl?
Did you use glue?

            Oneness of
glass cabochon—
caught our camera light

9. *The Boat Man*

Still harbor, that old mistake
to read the world, (human-scale)

On first qualities: great stillness,
vacuum, open on each side,
irregular as stone contemplation

Contrary: movement, beauty requires
flicker, we say, "transient," a wave we
watch but lose.

On Air.

Medieval Lovers: A Book of After-lives

darkness is a requirement of afterimages,
light is a requirement of afterimages

You know it like the back
of your speckled egg

made to encase nothing
in good company of millions

you and me
in the noise
and riot of mitosis

sore truth of cellular division
its weird way to thrive
   stupid source code
   dirty protein
   demented configuration

drowned mice relax sphincters in heaven
chemical compounds make hell a home
   their strange attractors
   push time against reversal
or let's not indulge *choice*

It's too much toward
how we know to define, or
define to know?

and the lapsed sample can't be used—
no longer relevant, can't show arc

of the germinal narrative, its bloom,
its love, starvation, its pouch
sealed off. Did you know, like us, it can
live in the past?
                    Memoir, glorification, method.

I address you: love, dear love
if we put your tool box on wheels,
it's not so heavy.
Your crown feathers dare beauty.
You are set off
by distance, distinct this season.
Come here. No need for a tannery now.
What will we do with half-round files?
Or those lathe parts
having shaped so much?

A tapered sort of philosophic edge,
an error that bugs you. Womb. A movie
has no scent. We miss the movie house,
that moldy-seated, popcorn-strewn
mouth for wolves and lambs together
in a portmanteau sort of enclosure.

Irresistible: moves bear-like
on stout legs. Why does our savannah
inheritance reduce all to silhouette
against open expanse? It pleases
the eye, satisfied safety protocol
a moment before our heads are taken off.
Spoke through evolution, right from the hub.
Golden grass and lion-like spear-carriers
flatten butchery, mark body decoration
with portable philosophy. See fetal practice

on monitors supplied by marriage
of science and business.

      It rains. It begins to track
whatever we do.

On the accidental disposal of artwork mistaken for litter

zombie after-lives
of lost novels, poetry
left behind in a taxi,
paintings secluded
behind walls, covered
over with banal
images, calendars,
buried in contiguity, decline,
woven into nests, burrows,
stitched, torn, resinous,
sunk, unburied again.

*

liquid relic, stress the secular
side in this narrative—elemental seas,
secular after-lives,
germinal thought

*

After-lives

*

Sabotage of seas, song
of polystyrene. Cereal aggression
its red plastic end-game.
Bend or alter what it finds:
tail fins, lenses, breach
with heat; force the shell.

*

Resurrected from cultural
dispossession—conquest,
money. Furnace of
pastoral returns.

*

The movie, a survey
of Russian cryogenic
research—half-Marx,
half-cat re-animation.
Flex-topian
filial duty via liquid
nitrogen-filled dewar.

*

Photos of cosmos,
maps it onto consciousness, or plants
intelligence in lurid language.

Historic assignment. Re-stated obscurity.
Things there then
not there. Corruption, vanishings, melt.

*

Here's the regal one who is all discourse,
isn't a slaughtered mirage or
recovered Birth of objects.
Words pronounced
are subordinate phantom—

*

                Of azure.
Thin bond of precision, a sort
of laughter: says "yes"
to Truth, to existence.
Talk-talk of myna birds
we work deep clasp
in our machine, ordinary
storehouse.

*

shape of bird: flight requires shape
shape of fish: swimming requires shape
lounge about can accommodate shapelessness

Zorn's Lemma

*

frontal presentation, drapes
opened—subject to force
of history. Spectacle
as completion of religious
fervor, political conquest,
monetary mountains.
A traveling salesman
tempts a pretty girl.

*

peacock, heron pair, ape
in a cape—
pursuit of love

unswerving devotion:
I waited for you
to serve a term,
hated your jailer,
taped shut the dam.

*

farm and country festivals
once
monetized under one tent
with
general surveillance made it
so
nothing has ever happened
here, nothing will.

*

described president's lawyers
as "freaks of law"

dolmens
two uprights and a capstone
government of forces

*

On double movements
and rotary blades,
centripetal tendency?
Stately couples stroll
arm in arm

*

On jungle velvet:
nature and properties, its
competence, erotic suit.
From his blue tunic
breath expands. Prepare
that curved horn for
audience: eaglets
in a downpour.

*

love in a time of panic—
on slopes burned down
to forever-chemicals, egg
cases form by the million;
in spurts, lovers spawn
resurrection.

*

We've melted monuments,
de-materialized our command
crew. We are eye-level to face
defaced by spray paint.
Metal coins carry them away.

*

fake poetry
desert poetry
mountain poetry
biomorphic poetry
grid poetry
collective poetry

*

Hold the Pick.
Shine the Panes.
Long-handled tool—
symmetrical! Transformed
mineral cleared "for later."
Buffed, not wiped.

*

An enclosing wall
for two lovers—paradise
or carpet-motif? Formal
hedge, pruned tree,
fitted vegetation, open
to sky of what time?

*

Could this produced
Book of Days be
about itself? How it
acts upon itself. Am I
Mediator of Displacement?
It makes itself,
afflicts the page, carbonized
mystic ego—

*

snowshoe
pistachio
aureole
gotta go

*

whispering words
shower scene
what a Complex! his father
was a Cubist, his mother
published "Concept of Man."
When he forged new art,
he did.

*

Sure: past the turnstile
by the data dump. Velvet
alienation.
A grid of streets: people hold
an idea of their city.
Neither created nor destroyed.

*

A day for butterflies on the move, but
for moths: summer nights. Phantom
pain, zombie after-life.

*

                    Lovers
under fennel,
recessional hymn.
It's up to us now.
Hounds after hares—
speculative principle,
no guarantee of what
comes next.

*

Slept on
clothing wadded in trash
bags. Resuscitated freedom
ramshackle if you look at Khan's
"No Go Backs".

*

We're in a basin.
Wash us with generalizations.
Sew ritual to our sleeve,
make a mountain of objects
no longer serving.

*

No words added
to color-field. Eremitic
monks stay-in-place,
kids levitate in caves,
and dogs, well, dogs
they are. Curled bronze
page, heavy unscripted age,
perforated remainder.

*

By May 15th, wild mustard
taller than people, fully
leafed oak. Shimmer
without being obsessed by
fact.

*

Helps lovers sleep,
cats dream, computer
files nest, parabolic
Lenten abstentions
slake.
Over done, too much time
under slack string slides.
Would you?

*

"Whoa, whoa, whoa ..."
sings the punk-rocker next
door, cooled from his travel
to now-cancelled concert
gigs. Hours of practice
keep musicians ready;
although there are examples:
those who put down instruments
for years then play
just like it was yesterday.

*

RV's circle their wagons
for air-conditioned camp outs
—lower Jawbone Canyon
Road. Hills scarred by
ORV's, target practice,
long-lasting scars.

*

You could circle your wagon
concisely as it's shadowed
through memory or Memorial
Day pit fires. Fuel getting
gone under carbon "by other
means," a hatch to older
skies close to serpentine
rubble cooled in geologic time.

*

        Or that
small planet with gravity
so weak you could get
a running start, leap into space,
be gone forever. Don't forget
your keys!
Fields of action and contemplation
climb out windows
left open.

*

Blank calendar alternately emptied
then filled without you.
People emerge with warm
weather, find niches
here and there usually
vacant. Seventeen-year
cicadas down South:
all about drive and mud
tubes, resurrection, song.

*

It's time to escape Medieval
frames, too ornate, too self-
destructive, too hysterical,
a border around a bomb.
Look for plain lined
paper, no frame, no supporting
argument, a thinness to burn.

*

South Rim, mesh steel
holder, three devices
and two conceits. Rusted
bolt, nut, flange: three
heavy pounds of former use.
Directory, environment,
appearance—things
come up next week.

*

They couldn't keep out a butterfly,
reminder of freedom.
Air currents' "evidence."

In the zombie mode of taxidermy:
boas, leopard skin vest,
Biblical sheep skin disguise.

Everyone a collector.

*

There is always "more" for
networks to cover.

How avant-gardism became
a conversion project. Not what
it was. Its sharp edges worn,
domesticated, Linked-in.

How luxury items
drew on retroactive life
as antiquities.

*

woes of the contact-tracer

how publication was baptism
in a river—some were held down
longer than others.

*

Hey, log. Hey, fallen tree.
My ingenious caress,
mycelium to your root tips,
to your underground shift.

Decomposition: starlight
arrives from dead stars,
peels my eye with afterlives.

*

minimal segments of what
comes down to us as requiem—
requiem: capacious field
recordings, wave of human

movement upon wave. Wave
upon wave.

torque fabric between mourning
and selfless gravity

*

It was as if all characters
in beatnik novels
found an afterlife.

"All adages are correct."

Did not remember a thing.

*

Three-part lines

line, forest way, stream way, how a work
        has begun, evident with color
                sound shape

once it's going further away, under
        the guise of departure points
                long gone, with expressly

contrary move from grid or grate, this
        time reclined along track and stanchion
                lines

anthers, speckled show when man doesn't
        show up to sign the lease, off-leash
                area, three words good-for-you,

not for me, green matter grouped apart, fermented
        to another life: gone, boulder on my chest,
                grieve a friend, gone

alcohol cooked out fast, incarnation carnation
        glide freely, improbable bird, brother above
                three bags below

peripheral dark escape, understory, leaf litter,
        under study, would have been here
                will home in on a scene

important to many of us, lead in what we sought
        backyard with a view, on-demand
                pleasure, efficiency-quotient

in a dark night crazed by Hanna-Barbera
        character pursuit of food, escape from
                brute strength, a Cunard luxury

liner, steam shovel, timecard, leashed
        dinosaur replete with parodic reference,
           workin' drone

taken away, take away: when your country
        does it to you, when you're done for,
           when it takes a man

ostrich farm conversion set apart, upended
        crust, belief in prayer, jazz, cool
             scene when we were young,

couldn't last, gone before we knew it, dance
        club jacket style freely swung, made
           with less, connected with two

hoses, one drain, one domain name kept it
        simply yours, washed with thin
           film of grit: we call it description,

that is, without emphasis the sun will come
        out, maybe not soon enough to ruin
           the ending, culprit, response

to flame pressed atmospherics any other
        way condensed, far from story,
           book, calendar, log, other

sequential inventions, music as expression
        of time, leaves on her own
           recognizance middle hot,

so hot, crank passenger window down, needle
    rises as we speed up, pre-digital,
        riddled with it, who was

he who was her best friend, laugh with mouth
    partly covered, search continues,
        literary smut, blue collected:

bodies, crew, is meaning a performance, ocean
    a noisy place, we swam the migrant-
        crossing, what could solidarity mean

without change, a dry spot, just standing?
    passengers toward a layered device
        near desired filament, loaded with

referential matter, is life made of ducks'
    scram behind willows, over-read
        movement as threat, message

of singular life absent religiosity, want, defined
    by emphatic question, that form,
        invented response made sexy

by leer, background hum of gravitational waves,
    can exit but there's no place to go,
        put an extraneous flourish on

immortality made difficult by direct action, organ-
    packed cavity we carried cashless where
        brackets were manufactured

that held up capital extraction moved offshore,
    vacant space, material always about itself,
        instrument for projection, made for

leveled possibility: people counting, seen
        and heard, sentence that got lost in thought,
            detective show, enigmatic motive,

vowel resonant substrate, drum, torso of earth
        hard to distinguish personal from historic
          reference in literary line,

former lover or French grad school poem, our youth,
        concocted images that haven't already
          existed in film, literature, comics,

horror of dying with everything complete, beauty
        of unfinished script: soon our fox will
          open the carcass for us ravens, eyes

already gone from the master narrative, disputation
        a mere refinement of joint effort,
          our ensemble cast separated

a weak one: aged, lame metaphor—can austere
        sculpture save our experiment in
          democracy, can bare theatre life,

cushioned sequence came to town, fell into
        present time in concho-belted skirt
          peasant blouse refinement,

similarity had simple rules, complex to obey,
        over-ripe fruit, invention of first days,
          origin as un-mythic as stone,

last chance tourism near glacial limit, inexplicable
        how more office towers are built over
          vacancy and forest fire smoke,

and worse: actually very explicable motive,
        roses behind deer fencing, extremely
                beige comedy, return to primal

wound as if a re-design could be drawn, restore
        clouds, suture vessel we shipped out on,
                cool a self-inflicted fever here.

Western Mycology

Sage scent competed with rain:
intermittent then recessional, familiar

mapped onto strange, heat-scent
of ironed sheets and shirts: all

fade out to homey tv console dust.

*"Thought of
bee that flew straight out from polluted
burrow that might collapse if we don't
keep writing:*

*Somehow, we are unreadable charms of
this planet."*

Set facts on the loose from larger
interpretive fame, help on the way

it sounds like a story, but empty
placeholders are unknowable—

disrupted delivery, mountain roads
old dozer in weeds starts up after

four decades in a puff of exhaust,
yee-hah, whereas machinery stalled

here, may have felt side effects,
flu-like, short-lived, hyphenated.

Don't we like our return to phrasal
time, something we can dance to,

big country, small ethos, good thing
we have pre-computer, talented stunt

riders, force of culture, a rare free time
scission of pigeon color cones

spotting for prize specimen each summer
life aboard, harpoon in the old way

expectation of the catch, swagger
of boss who tamed nature, shortened

span of diverse biome, no triumph
in litigation against children, monument

of literary knowledge, metropole outpost
here, second last receipt for arrival of

animatronic means of historic
depiction colored by time, shaped

by collective force of little particles,
then stepped out to conduct ocean waves

brass comes in, strings retreat, no
more obvious crash than right here

against a grand boulder, socio-historic,
cymbal-mounted, Indo-European language,

recovered work split across this spine
a knuckle to ride against, saddle blanket

first, then propositional strap, dry grass.
Five runners pass in step as one

beautiful animal, trail hormonal
cloud, resonators:

wave, sea spray, a more universal
urchin. Electric smell in lightening

storm, by evening: spicy desert plants
advance from moisture-shift, show

off "altogether-now." Memory-
instigator, chlorophyll, mushroom

moisture, nerve transmitter relayed
bulb to brain, where continents fall away.

Spring Lines

Configure me near lenticular attraction

more of it, response to beatings, carved keep,

scrapped out hulk made a name for itself,

satellite mapped snow depth, prelude

envelope—climbing vine Persephone turn:

it all comes

up, not every accumulation in the novel of experience

bends toward change (maturity, deterioration, etc.) in our

protagonist. But, in the right hands, our reader morphs,

ambiguity as the underlying condition of love,

representation always falling short of rain itself,

sampled worlds and selves mere museum pieces

or poems, not commercially prepared slides

for narrow hallways. In each other's arms,

came into acceleration at lift-off, an idea

of futurity off to the side, treasure dusted

off to present in a fair light, hospital time

drive at dawn along flood-control channel,

circulating coin of fluid dynamics,

supply towns congregated toward

tower, at-grade rail, power stanchions

stitched a topographic contour, chalk lines

snapped briskly: we have our guide to

the stairs, to the stars, dirt and ditches

corrugated toward power, skimming

scam, billing fraud, sold from car trunk,

ambition for two hours at a time, line up

line down, storm torn, three bags full,

four fortunates flee: ah, frugal again

illegally occupying space, so called,

test strip of property, unlisted, in play:

artist's acquisition, section map,

fallen tree milled to potential use, yes,

we belong here, sort of, oil our body,

of flirt and estate, acrostic vertical

long-stem iris, gravity of mother,

shadowed

bodies

film shoot wrapped the block, truant

ordered to live with grandparents named

gaffer and coil, put away, up at night.

ACKNOWLEDGMENTS

Portions of earlier versions of *Bumblebees* appeared in *BathHouse Journal* (Eastern Michigan University, Ryan Cox, editor), as an online chapbook with artwork by Geoffrey Gatza (BlazeVOX [books], Geoffrey Gatza, editor), in *Poetry from Instructions, A Work of (Non-Combinatory) Generative Poetry* (Sophical Things: Los Angeles, Guy Bennett et al, editors), in *Pamenar Press Online Magazine* (Kess Mohammedi, editor), in *Journal of Poetics Research* (John Tranter, editor), and forthcoming in *Texas Review* (Ginger Ko, editor). "The Curiosities of Janice Lowry" is in response to the catalog for *The Curiosities of Janice Lowry*, an exhibition of the late artist Janice Lowry's assemblage and other visual art works published for CSUF Grand Central Art Center in Santa Ana, CA, presented 7 May–12 June, 2011.

An excerpt from "Medieval Lovers: A Book of After-lives" and "On the accidental disposal of artwork mistaken for litter" was performed as part of *Broadcast from Home* by Lisa Bielawa, composer with "Works & Process at the Guggenheim," Zoom (July 16, 2020 at 7:30pm ET). Archived as "WPA Virtual Commissions: Lisa Bielawa's "Broadcast from Home" - Chapter 15 "After-lives": https://www.youtube.com/watch?v=dDVkanVChLE and here: https://www.lisabielawa.net/broadcast-from-home

A later segment was included in Week One of *Broadcast From Here* by Lisa Bielawa, http://www.lisabielawa.net/bfh-radio-broadcast-from-here (March 2021).

Note: The composition of "Medieval Lovers: A Book of After-lives" and "On the accidental disposal of artwork mistaken for litter" involved, in part, writing on pages in *Medieval Lovers: A Book of Days* (Weidenfeld & Nicolson, 1988), a commercially produced "blank book" that includes pictures (paintings, frescoes, mirror case, etc.) and troubadour poetry from medieval sources as well as heavily decorated borders on the blank pages of its weekly calendar. My entries crossed daily events, listening to talks, music, film and video art, reading from philosophy, art history, lefty political critique, and contemporary poetry. I was interested in an interview statement by artist Robert Morris on the accidental disposal of one of his artworks mistaken for litter: that even in the trash, it is still art, and even if it is taken into burrows and fields by animals, it is still art. How can that be?

Thanks to all.

ROOF BOOKS
the best in language since 1976

Recent & Selected Titles

- HAND ME THE LIMITS by Ted Rees, 130 pp. $20
- TGIRL.JPG by Sol Cabrini, 114 pp. $20
- SECRET SOUNDS OF PONDS by David Rothenberg, 138 pp. $29.95
- THE POLITICS OF HOPE (After the War) by Dubravka Djurić, translated by Biljana D. Obradović, 148 pp. $25
- BAINBRIDGE ISLAND NOTEBOOK by Uche Nduka, 248 pp. $20
- MAMMAL by Richard Loranger, 128 pp. $20
- FOR TRAPPED THINGS by Brian Kim Stefans, 138 pp. $20
- EXCURSIVE by Elizabeth Robinson, 140 pp. $20
- I, BOOMBOX by Robert Glück, 194 pp. $20
- TRUE ACCOUNT OF TALKING TO THE 7 IN SUNNYSIDE by Paolo Javier, 192 pp. $20
- THE NIGHT BEFORE THE DAY ON WHICH by Jean Day, 118 pp. $20
- MINE ECLOGUE by Jacob Kahn, 104 pp. $20
- SCISSORWORK by Uche Nduka, 150 pp. $20
- THIEF OF HEARTS by Maxwell Owen Clark, 116 pp. $20
- DOG DAY ECONOMY by Ted Rees, 138 pp. $20
- THE NERVE EPISTLE by Sarah Riggs, 110 pp. $20
- QUANUNDRUM: [i will be your many angled thing] by Edwin Torres, 128 pp. $20
- FETAL POSITION by Holly Melgard, 110 pp. $20
- DEATH & DISASTER SERIES by Lonely Christopher, 192 pp. $20
- THE COMBUSTION CYCLE by Will Alexander, 614 pp. $25

More information on titles
can be found at Roofbooks.com

To order, please go to
Roofbooks.com